This Gift

is for

____

from

____

Lasting
Love

THOMAS NELSON PUBLISHERS
Nashville

Unless otherwise noted, all Scripture quotations are from the NEW KING JAMES VERSION of the Bible. Copyright © 1979, 1980, 1982, Thomas Nelson, Inc., Publishers.
Published in Nashville, Tennessee, by Janet Thoma Books, a division of Thomas Nelson, Inc., Publishers, and distributed in Canada by Word Communications, Ltd., Richmond, British Columbia, and in the United Kingdom by Word (UK), Ltd., Milton Keynes, England.

Printed in Singapore

1 2 3 4 5 6—
98 97 96 95 94 93

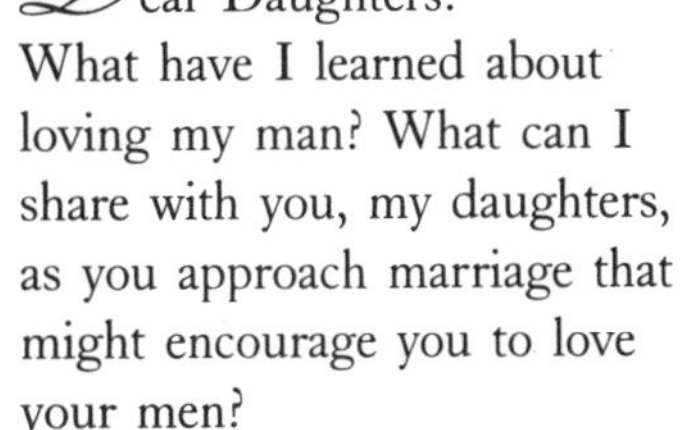

Dear Daughters:
What have I learned about loving my man? What can I share with you, my daughters, as you approach marriage that might encourage you to love your men?

Beginning today, I will write you letters and share with you all I've been learning about developing an intimate oneness with my lover and best friend.

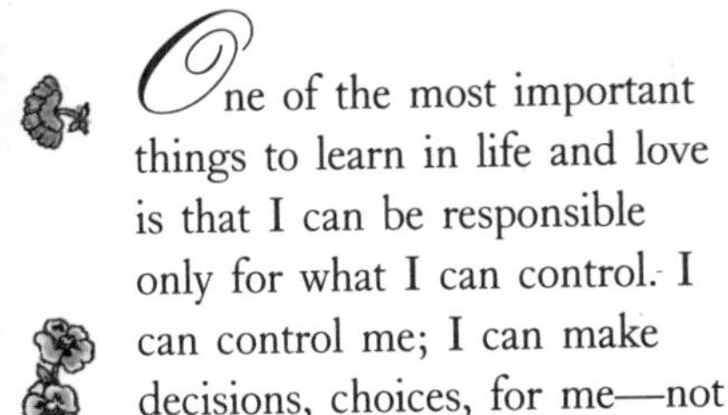

One of the most important things to learn in life and love is that I can be responsible only for what I can control. I can control me; I can make decisions, choices, for me—not for my husband.

Since I am responsible for myself, I can learn daily to make the choices that will lead me toward my goal of being a godly wife.

Life is a series of choices, most of them so small we usually don't even realize that we're making them or why, but their cumulative effect is more powerful than we can imagine.

An intimate oneness is built by the daily choices we make. You must choose to love your man, or your lack of choice will lead you in the opposite direction.

To learn to love your unique man, you must understand his needs.

The Bible best explains our needs in Genesis 2. We both have the need for intimacy and for companionship.

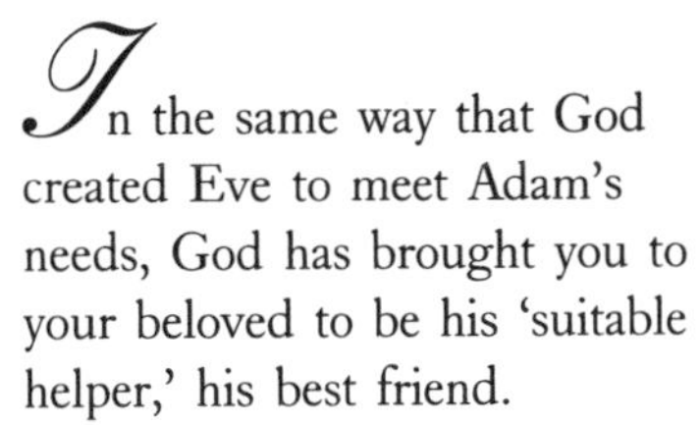

In the same way that God created Eve to meet Adam's needs, God has brought you to your beloved to be his 'suitable helper,' his best friend.

What is a best friend?

'One who comes in when the whole world has gone out.'

God proclaimed that the one who would be your best friend would also be your lover.

Your marriage ceremony is just the beginning. Growing and becoming one flesh takes a lifetime of making daily choices to really love your man.

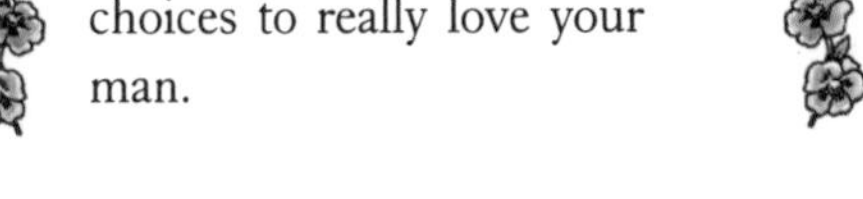

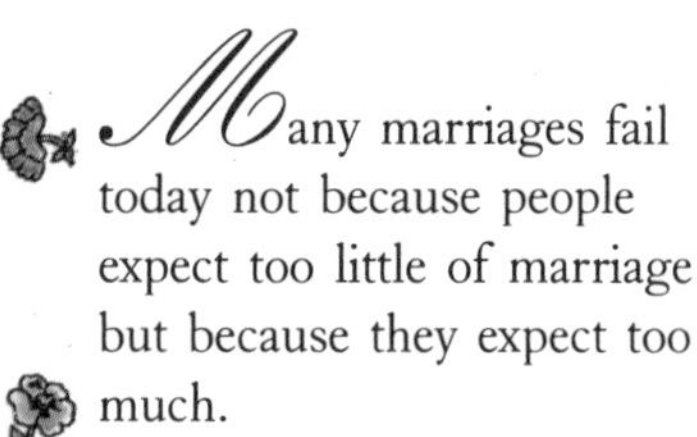

Many marriages fail today not because people expect too little of marriage but because they expect too much.

A good marriage is not one where perfection reigns; it is a relationship where a healthy perspective overlooks a multitude of "unresolvables."

The more you understand your husband's uniqueness, the more you understand his deep needs, which allows you to meet those needs.

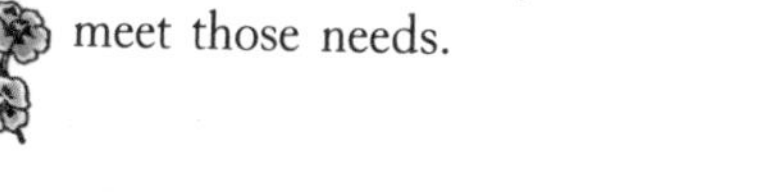

Marriage is the adventure of discovering each other so you might deeply share an intimacy of the soul, body, and spirit.

What your husband needs will be a reflection of his longing for companionship, intimacy, and significance.

How his needs will be demonstrated will be unique. You must make it your project to study your man.

In studying him, listen to him, talk to him, and get so bold as to ask him how he would describe his five greatest needs.

You need to accept your husband unconditionally.

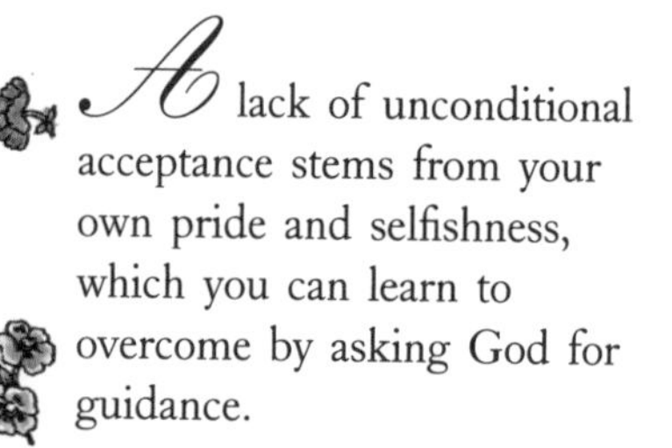

A lack of unconditional acceptance stems from your own pride and selfishness, which you can learn to overcome by asking God for guidance.

We are all constantly changing and growing. Be ready to accept these changes and the growth of intimacy that will result.

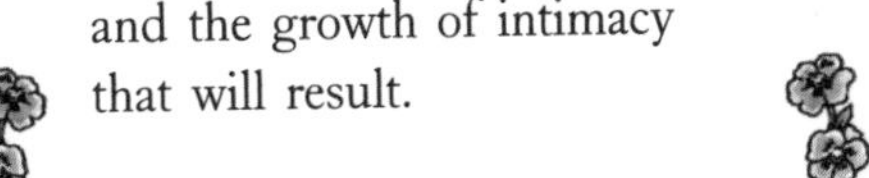

Encouragement is the kind of expression of love that helps your husband become all God desires him to be, and it helps develop his potential.

Only you know his deepest needs, his vulnerability, and his hidden weakness. You also know his potential as a man, his areas of talent and his hidden strength.

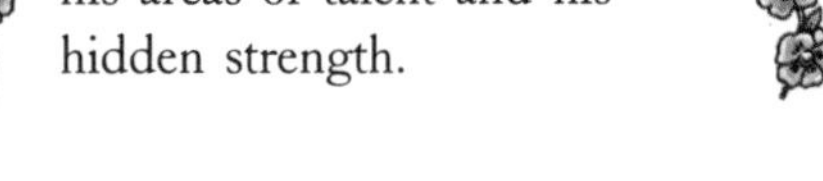

Encouragement has great power, but so does discouragement.

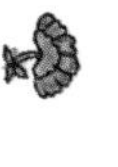

Emerson said, "Beware of what you set your mind on for that you will surely become."

Right thinking begins by controlling your thoughts.

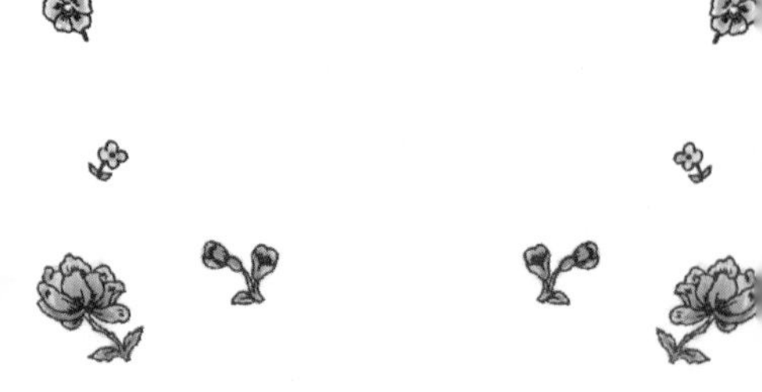

You need to be in control of your mind and make the conscious choice to think about life and your husband from God's perspective and seek to encourage him.

"For as a man thinks in his heart, so *is* he."

—Prov. 23:7

Right thinking leads to right words, which leads to right actions, which becomes encouragement to your man.

Love is silence when your words might hurt. Love is praise when your words might help.

To encourage your man and develop intimacy, you need to communicate well with each other.

Good communication begins by learning to listen effectively when your beloved is talking.

Real listening is receiving and accepting what your man is saying plus seeking to understand what he really means.

Commit to memory the verse from James 1:19, "Let everyone be swift to hear, slow to speak, slow to wrath."

You must communicate what your husband is doing that hurts or irritates you in a loving way . . . not in anger.

Express your thoughts, feelings, and ideas to your husband using "I" messages instead of "you" messages.

A lover-best friend intimacy cannot grow without time to talk.

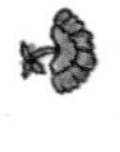

Deep communication will not always just happen, but it will happen much more often if we are together frequently.

The most intimate part of your marriage will be your sexual relationship.

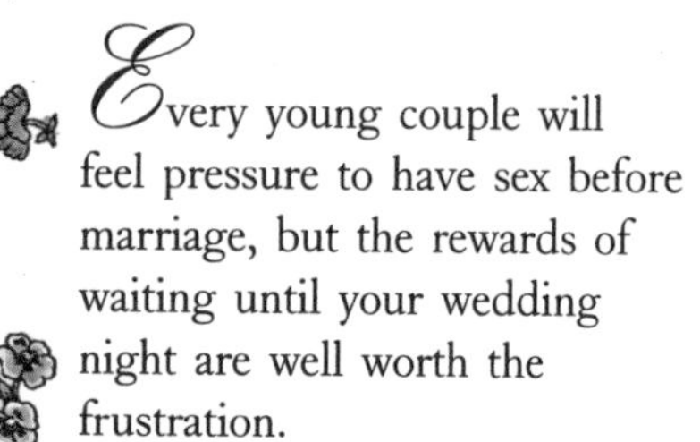

Every young couple will feel pressure to have sex before marriage, but the rewards of waiting until your wedding night are well worth the frustration.

Contrary to what we see in movies and on television, sex is not always natural and perfect. Nothing in marriage happens instantly.

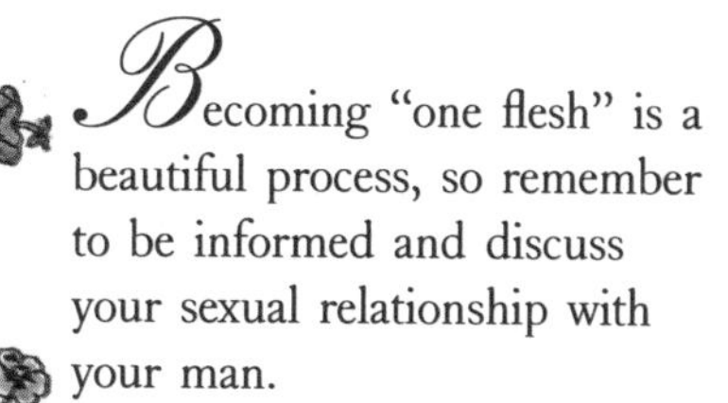

Becoming "one flesh" is a beautiful process, so remember to be informed and discuss your sexual relationship with your man.

Sex is not a competitive sport. It is a discovery of intimacy between you and your mate.

God gave the gift of sex for you to create life, for an intimate oneness, for pleasure, and for comfort.

In lovemaking, there is beautiful intimacy, but there should also be fun, laughter, joy, and variety.

Anything is okay as long as you both agree. Sex is God's gift to His people, so use it wisely.

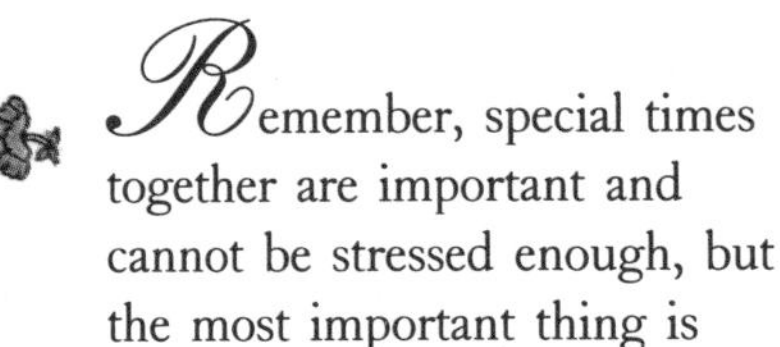

Remember, special times together are important and cannot be stressed enough, but the most important thing is your attitude.

Whether you are aware of it or not, your attitude is projected; your man senses either your love or your rejection.

Sex, like supper, loses much of its flavor when it becomes totally predictable.

Having a creative sexual relationship means to bring into existence a vital and invigorating perspective.

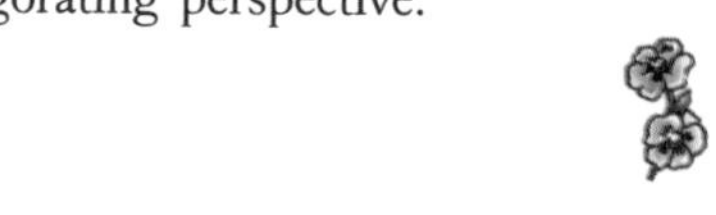

One reason people miss out on beauty in sex is that they do not choose to make time to spend together with their lovers.

Loving each other should be a priority.

Remember that giving your body to your husband is to give him the greatest gift intended by God for intimacy.

While it may sound logical for each partner to say, "You do your part, and I'll do mine," this idea will lead to disappointment.

God's plan for marriage is a 100/100 plan based on how Jesus lived His life.

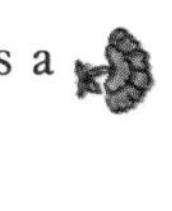

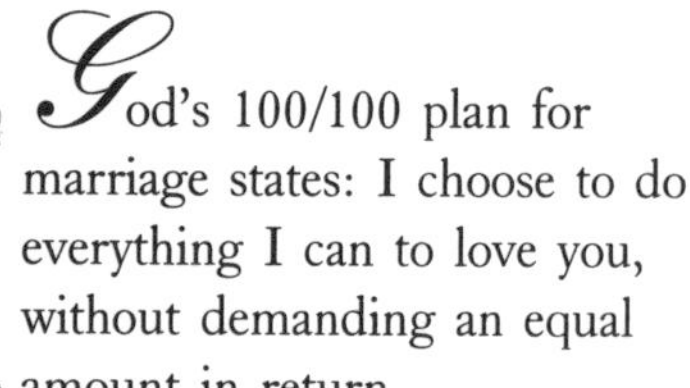

God's 100/100 plan for marriage states: I choose to do everything I can to love you, without demanding an equal amount in return.

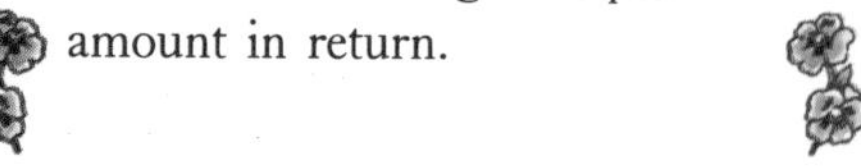

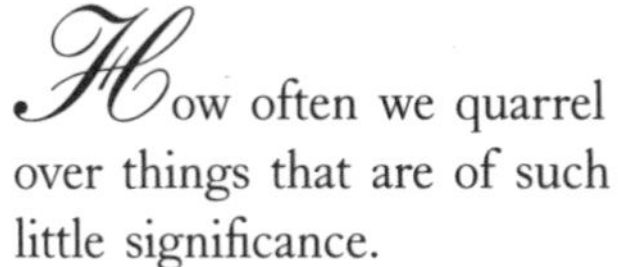

How often we quarrel over things that are of such little significance.

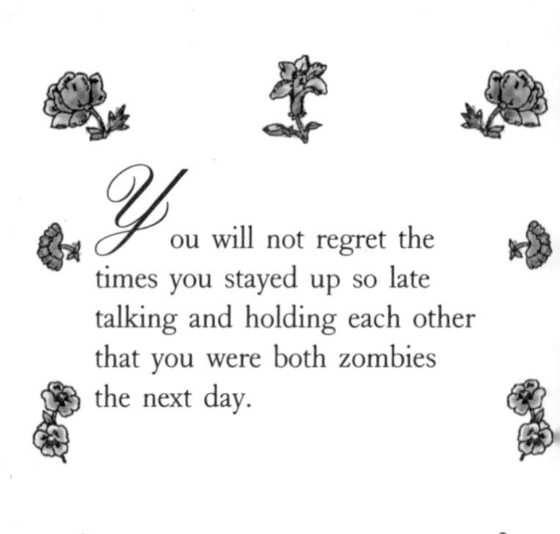

You will not regret the times you stayed up so late talking and holding each other that you were both zombies the next day.

But you will regret the thousands of hours that you spent fighting over nothing.

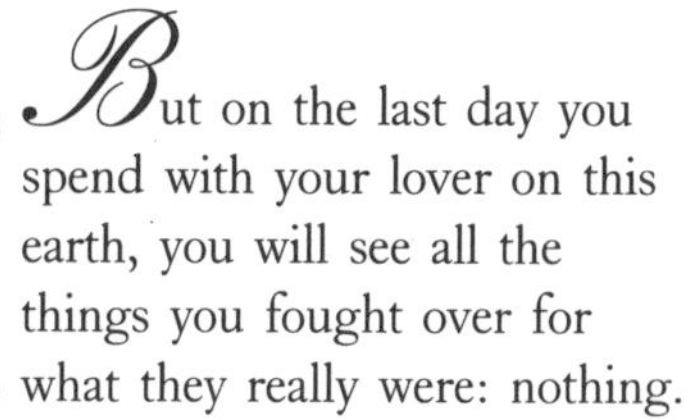

But on the last day you spend with your lover on this earth, you will see all the things you fought over for what they really were: nothing.

Love is learning to say I'm sorry often, learning to swallow pride and selfishness, and learning to forgive.

A happy marriage is the union of two good forgivers who have committed to not hold a grudge.

To learn to love and forgive we must choose with our free will to forgive.

We must also forget the person's sin, never naming it again.

Seal your forgiveness with your behavior, demonstrating love with tender-hearted kindness.

An eternal perspective is viewing your marriage and what is important from God's perspective.

To live each day in light of time is to realize that love is a gift from God, and that this man beside you is a gift.

No matter how many years we have to grow in our intimate oneness, the time is short.

We are daily people, not lifetime people, but God wants us to be eternal people. Look beyond the routine of life and realize life while we live it.

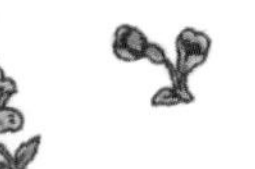

The minutes of marriage pass so quietly, so consistently, that we fail to realize the time is ticking away.

We can't bring back time, but we can seize the opportunity today to live each day as a gift of God: seeking to love, seeking to encourage, seeking to give, seeking excellence.

My daughters, for you, for me, I desire that we will not only be able to live with ourselves, but that we will live with peace and joy knowing that we have made the choices that build an intimate oneness with our husbands.

I love you,
Mom

This is what it means to serve, to minister, to give. Of course, both partners must strive to be 100 percent.

Daily we receive messages from society to be selfish and to have things our way.

We must choose to be faithful and loving, not because of what we will get in return, but because God has asked us to be this way.

The most difficult time to be loving is in a time of crisis.

In regard to marriage, I would like to define crisis as "a situation that has reached a critical phase; an unstable phase; a crucial time."

The world is realistic and marriage is not all fun and games.

Part of maturity is realizing that negative as well as positive circumstances are part of life and marriage.

In crisis there is either the danger that we will let the crisis destroy our oneness or the opportunity that our oneness will grow deeper and more beautiful through the trial.

The temptation is to withdraw from each other and try to handle our hurts, thus becoming self-centered.

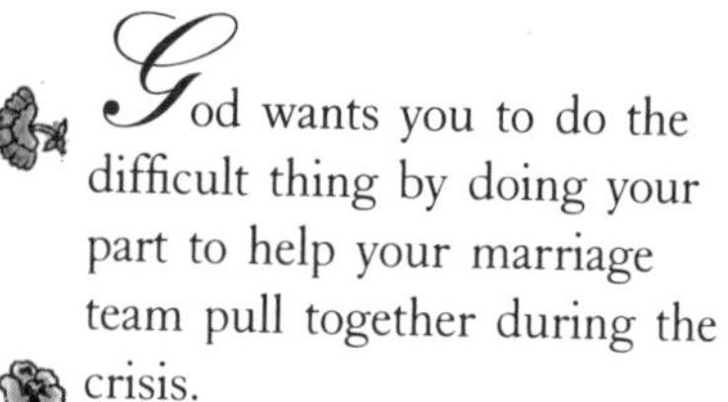

God wants you to do the difficult thing by doing your part to help your marriage team pull together during the crisis.

During your crisis, try to get away from the problem for a while so the two of you can relax, forget the problem temporarily, and love each other.

This escape suggestion helps you to clear your eyes of the problem and on to God's working in the midst of the mess.

You will make mistakes in your marriage. When you do, you have two options.

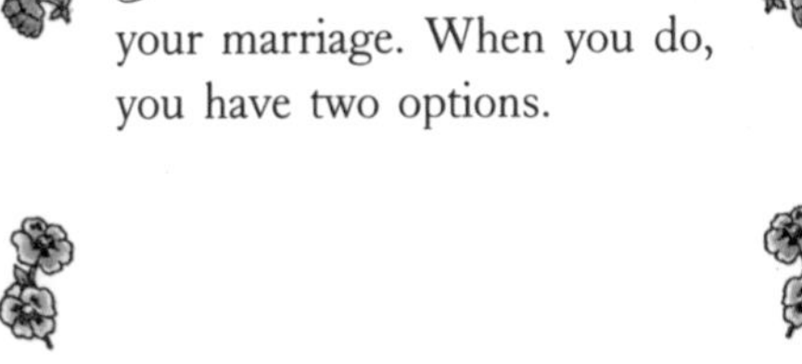

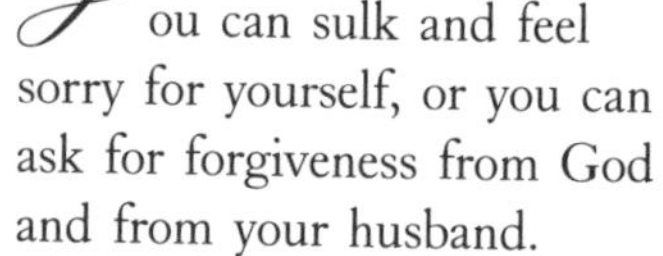

You can sulk and feel sorry for yourself, or you can ask for forgiveness from God and from your husband.

When we ask for forgiveness, we admit our wrong and only ours.

We confess, then forget, and move on asking God for strength and power with a new determination to make wise choices, even when our emotions scream to do otherwise.